How to Draw Pixel Art

A Simplified and Intuitive Approach to Drawing Pixel

Characters

by Hina Tno

Copyright Notes

Table of Contents

Introduction

Welcome to an incredible adventure called Pixel Art! Get ready to explore a colorful world where imagination meets technology. In this journey, you'll become a digital artist and create amazing pictures using tiny squares called pixels. Pixels are like magical building blocks that you can arrange on a special computer program or app. Just imagine having a virtual canvas where you can place each pixel to bring your ideas to life. With a simple click or a tap, you can create anything you can dream of – from cute animals to beautiful landscapes and even your favorite video game characters! You can even share it online, where people from all around the globe can admire your talent and be inspired by your creations.

Are you ready to embark on this exciting journey? Grab your digital paintbrush and let's dive into the fascinating world of Pixel Art, where your imagination has no limits!

Character 01

Stage 1

Begin by drawing the shapes of the head as a guideline.

Stage 2

For the face, add the shading to lovely eyes and lip as

depicted.

Stage 3

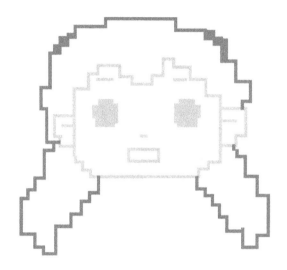

Then, for hairstyles, draw some fine lines.

Stage 4

Now add the curved line to form the hat as depicted.

Stage 5

Continue to add the shapes of the outfit as depicted.

Stage 4

Now add the curved line to form the hat as depicted.

Stage 5

Continue to add the shapes of the outfit as depicted.

Stage 6

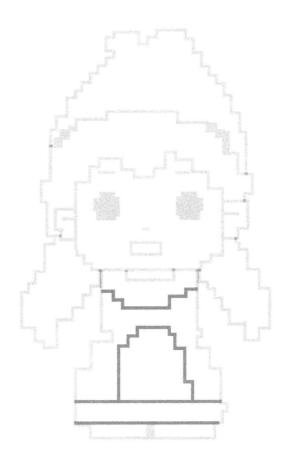

Then, refine the lines to create the features of the

outfit as depicted.

Stage 7

Now add the shapes of the hands and feet as shown in

thick lines.

Stage 8

And before concluding the pixel, add any guidelines.

Stage 9

Lastly, to complete the pixel, erase the drawing lines

and round the corners, as depicted in the sample.

Stage 10

Finally, color the pixel as guideline.

Character 02

Stage 1

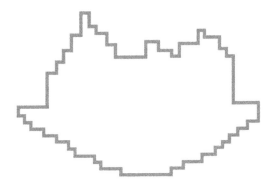

First, make a head out of simple shapes.

Stage 2

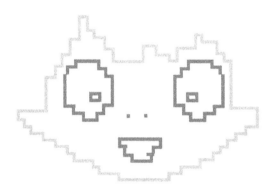

Next, define the lip and eye's form by adding the pupil

as depicted.

Stage 3

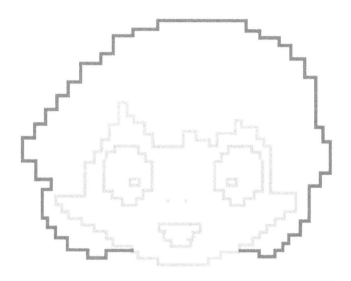

Then, add the curved form of the hirs as in thick lines.

Stage 4

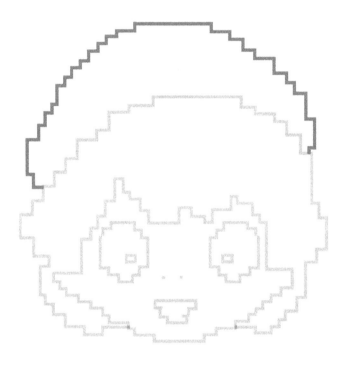

Continue to add more curved to the hat as shown.

Stage 5

Now add the shapes of the outfit as shown in thick lines.

Stage 6

Then, outline the curved lines to form the hands and

feet of the pixel as guideline.

Stage 7

And manage the pixel portion by adding details in the

thick line.

Stage 8

Lastly, to complete the pixel, erase the drawing lines

and round the shapes, as in the sample above.

Stage 9

Finally, color the pixel as guideline.

Character 03

Stage 1

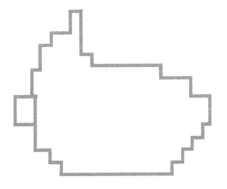

Start by drawing the shape of the face as depicted.

Stage 2

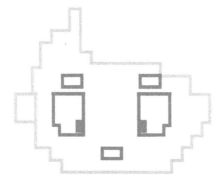

Next, outline the shapes of the eyes and mouth as

shown.

Stage 3

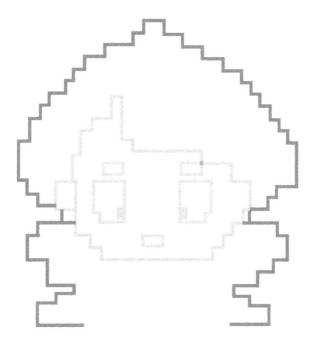

Then, draw the curved line to form the hair as shown in

thick line.

Stage 4

Now add the shapes of the outfit as shown thick lines.

Stage 5

Continue to outline the shapes of the lower portion as

guideline.

Stage 6

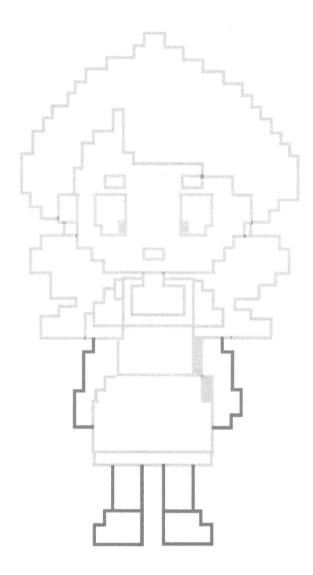

Then, add the shapes of the hands and feet as

guideline.

Stage 7

As a guideline, finish with thick lines to add further

details.

Stage 8

Lastly, erase any guidelines before finishing the pixel. As

necessary, redraw any outstanding drawing lines.

Stage 9

Finally, color the pixel as guideline.

Character 04

Stage 1

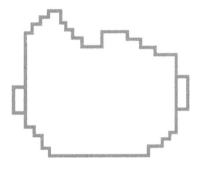

Begin by outlining the shape to form the hand as

depicted.

Stage 2

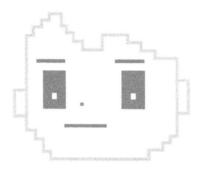

Next, draw the lines to round the eyes and mouth on the

face.

Stage 3

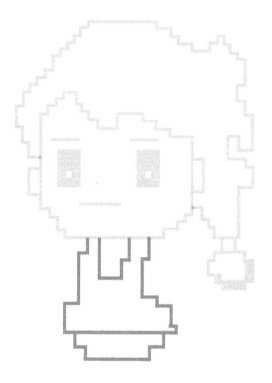

Then, outline the shapes of the outfit to the torso as

depicted.

Stage 4

Continue to refine more curved lines to form the pants

as guideline.

Stage 5

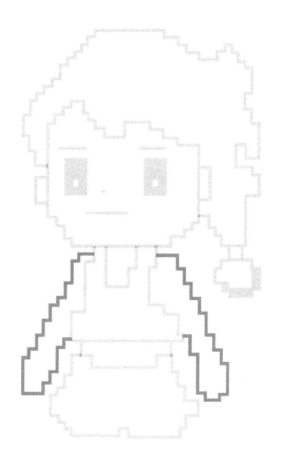

Now add the shapes to create the hands as shown in

thick lines.

Stage 6

Then, outline the shapes of the legs and feet form as

depicted.

Stage 7

And erase any guidelines before finishing and add in a

little more detail to the drawing.

Stage 8

Lastly, finish the pixel as shown in the sample above.

Stage 9

Finally, color the pixel as guideline.

Character 05

Stage 1

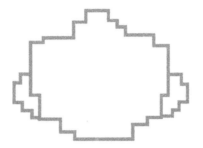

Start by drawing the shapes of the head as depicted.

Stage 2

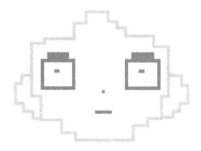

Next, draw the shapes round the eyes, nose and lip as

shown.

Stage 3

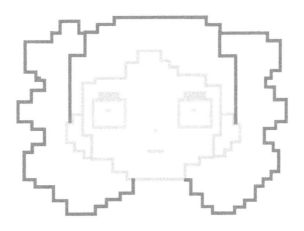

Then, draw the shapes of the hairs to the head as

depicted.

Stage 4

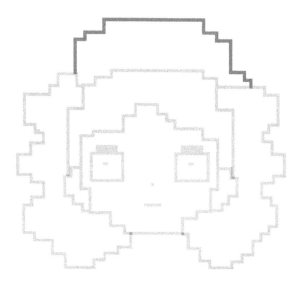

Continue to add more shape to the head as shown in

thick line.

Stage 5

Now outline the shapes of the outfit as shown.

Stage 6

Follow that, draw more shapes of the pants to the lower

portion as depicted.

Stage 7

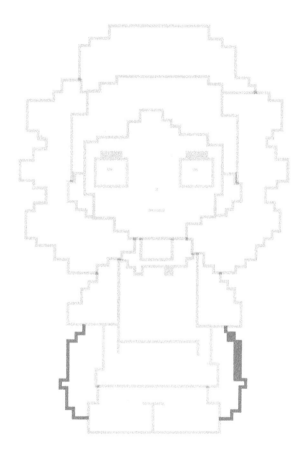

Then, add the curved lines to form the hand pattern as

shown.

Stage 8

Then, add the shapes for the legs and shoes to the feet

as guideline.

Stage 9

And eliminate the guides and round the edges as shown.

Stage 10

Lastly, add details to complete the pixel by remove the

guidelines. Redraw any final drawing lines as necessary.

Stage 11

Finally, color the pixel as guideline.

Character 06

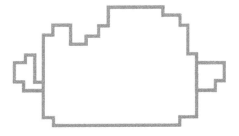

First, outline the shapes for the head as shown.

Stage 2

Next, outline the shapes of the eyes, nose and mouth as

depicted.

Stage 3

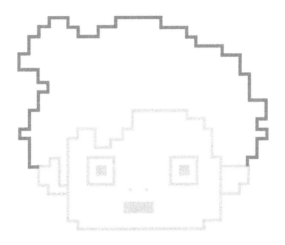

Then, outline more shapes of the hairs as depicted.

Stage 4

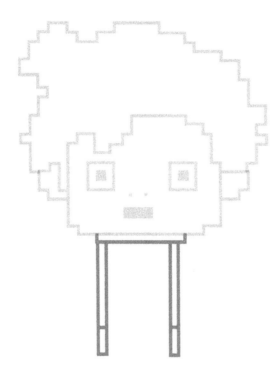

Now draw the lines to design the outfit features as

shown.

Stage 5

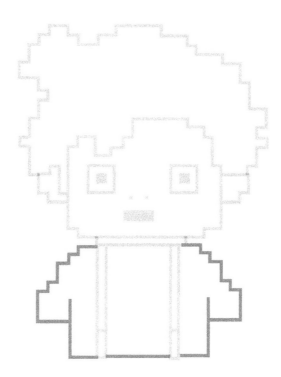

Continue to outline the shapes of the shirt as depicted.

Stage 6

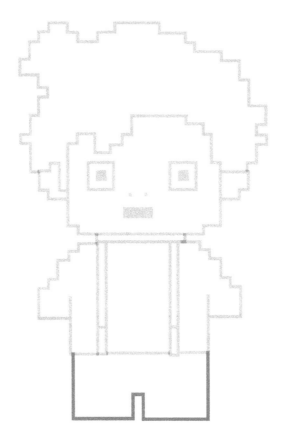

Then add more shapes of the pants as in thick lines.

Stage 7

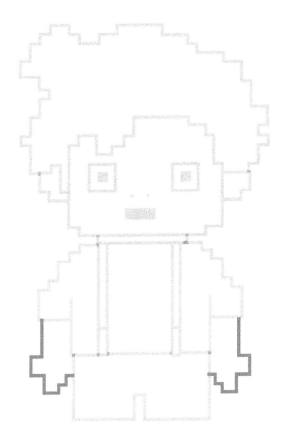

Follow that, outline the shapes of the hand form as

depicted.

Stage 8

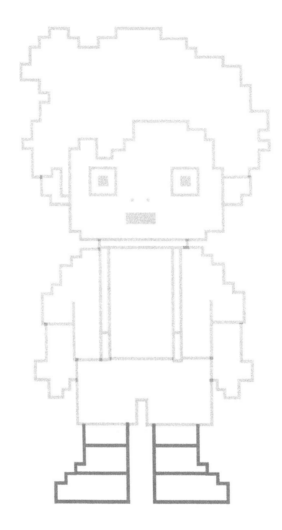

Then, add the lines for the legs and feet as shown in

thick lines.

Stage 9

And add any guidelines before completing the pixel.

Stage 10

Lastly, erase the drawing lines and round the corners,

as depicted in the sample.

Stage 11

Finally, color the pixel as guideline.

Character 07

Stage 1

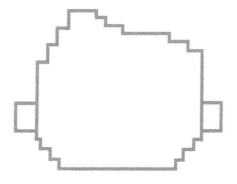

Begin by drawing the shapes of the head as depicted.

Stage 2

Next, outline the pupil of the eyes, lines of nose and lip

as shown.

Stage 3

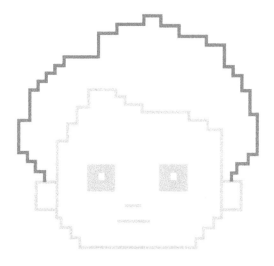

Then, draw the curved line for the hairstyle as shown.

Stage 4

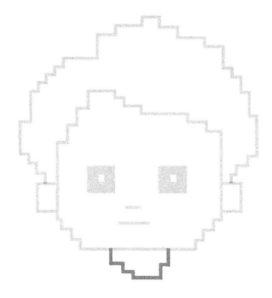

Now draw the line for the neck portion as depicted.

Stage 5

Then, outline the shapes of the shirt as guideline.

Stage 6

Continue to outline the shapes of the pants as depicted.

Stage 7

Then, draw the shapes of the hands in thick lines.

Stage 8

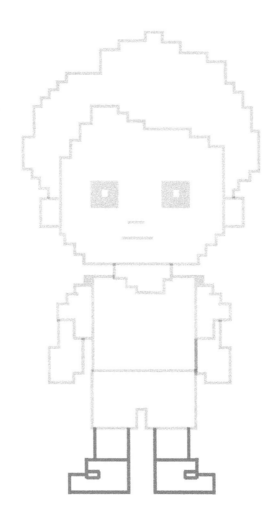

Follow that, outline the shapes of the legs and feet form

as depicted.

Stage 9

And manage the pixel portion by adding details in the

thick line.

Stage 10

Lastly, to complete the pixel, erase the drawing lines

and round the shapes, as in the sample above.

Stage 11

Finally, color the pixel as guideline.

Conclusion

Congratulations, young artist! You have completed an amazing journey into the wonderful world of Pixel Art. Throughout this adventure, you have learned how to use pixels as building blocks to create incredible artwork on a virtual canvas. You have discovered the joy of experimenting and mixing different colors to make your artwork truly unique. Let the world marvel at your talent and be inspired by your creations. Remember, Pixel Art is not just about the result, but also about the journey itself. Enjoy the process, have fun, and continue to explore your imagination through pixels. There are countless adventures waiting for you in the realm of art.

So, keep dreaming big, young artist! Let your creativity soar as you embark on new artistic endeavors. Whether it's through pixels, paint, or any other medium, the world is your canvas. You have the power to create beauty and make a lasting impact. Your journey into Pixel Art is just the beginning of an incredible artistic voyage!

Printed in the USA
CPSIA information can be obtained
at www.ICGtesting.com
LVHW070216260124
770044LV00030B/759